THE PROPAGANDA FACTORY,
OR SPEAKING OF TREES

MARC VINCENZ

SPUYTEN DUYVIL
NEW YORK CITY

ISBN 978-0-923389-05-5

Text by Marc Vincenz
Cover image *EarthMen* © Inga Maria Brynjarsdottir

Library of Congress Cataloging-in-Publication Data

Vincenz, Marc.
[Poems. Selections]
The propaganda factory : or, speaking of trees / Marc Vincenz.
pages cm
Poems.
ISBN 978-0-923389-05-5
I. Title.
PS3622.I538P76 2013
811'.6--dc23

2013005701

THE PROPAGANDA FACTORY,
OR SPEAKING OF TREES

Contents

POST NUCLEAR LOVE CHILD

She'd often say if you'd never lived through the war
you wouldn't sense the world as the fragile creature she is,

like the lone butterfly, the bird or the mouse
wagging tragically across all those blank distances.

& during the Blitz, blackout night after night
the family's sleep interred yet reinforced in rebar,

the sky falling in pieces as the radio crackled
White Cliffs of Dover & rain never left rainbows,
          not even on Sundays.

As a child, I imagined it was like listening to stars forming,
the creation of galaxies, a romantic notion which sizzled

out there in my own cranium. Normally, at this point he'd interject,
thick glasses resting stork-like on the end of his bent nose

like an afterthought; invariably he'd be glued to his Telegraph
as he vowed to be ahead of the Times; he'd say, Ah, the world

in metaphor, a mouse caught in the headlight of the solar glare,
no grandfather clock with its soothing tick-tock, no farmer's wife

with her carving knife, just millions of rodents scrapping
for a bite of heavenly paradise. Where the hell's that Pied Piper?

She'd roll her eyes in cosmic circles, then get on with knitting
woolly caps for the grandchild or niece, or even some old bat

roosting in the nursing home down the road.
Years later, it's too late to ask them about the war

they've gone quasar, dematerialised into the subatomic;
today a fifty-megaton mushroom cloud splutters plutonium

across a Soviet sea of ice, & a nude named Natasha
lies spent, flushed pink, dozing beside me,

as I stare into the dark, the world is surely a tragedy,
but outside a haze of butterflies flickers against the moon.

Speaking Of Trees

~

Ah, what an age it is / When to speak of trees is almost a crime…

—Berthold Brecht

For the Shadow Council,

history has no future it's more testament than tenacity
more tenement than transience

        an illusion of Earth standing on its head

like the old codger who collects
in the underpass connecting
      and the late cars squawking overhead

and what of the rusty cup and the mangy dog?

obligatory for a man who fights for poems by firelight

and she
   never once reincarnated

she who smells of forgetfulness and TV dinners

she who carries the cart to the hypermart for dented cans and cold cream

and he
   he with the scar under his left eye

the crewcut and the crescent and teardrop tattoo
always crying to the moon
always ready to die

and on the way home to the other side
   where beer was once served lukewarm

she   another she
          carries the touch of men's hair and fingers

filaments of inbreeding breathing through layers and skins

reeking of old men's fables
             of survivors and war heroes

and though their ghosts have vanished

             shadows still drag behind like bats
transmuting along the corridors

             swooping above flagpoles
lining the concourse
with their indelible silence

MONKEY BRAINS

We ate monkey brains in secrecy
just to see what they tasted like,
as if they might remind us of you;
and although the ancient custom
was to strap the chosen primate
in a made-for-measure cabinet
with only the shaved cranium exposed,
crush the skull-bone with a golden hammer,
while she screamed and whimpered,
begging for the beginning of time;
an experience, I've been told, like no other,
we proffered them fried in garlic and onions
separated from the body,
dipped them in rice wine vinegar.
You got sick after that, struggled
with fever for ten days and nights,
dampening the sheets with your toxins.
I knew you'd live.
You wanted to die.
I remember the morning your fever broke
was the morning the H5N1 virus
flamed across the country,
everyone was wearing a blue mask
and we no longer feared the secret police.

CONVEX

Mosaic of fly's eyes.
Compound light
in pixels. Pinpoints.
Water is nervous
un-distilled, refracted
strip-stressed colours
bent into meniscus,
goose-bumping.
When sun is served
days from now
I shall see you again
in a clean light.
Numbered.
In your own image.

BICYCLE

They say I have a face like a bicycle
       & I wonder if from the front or the side

       I guess it's a compliment since they ride them
along the canal & when the sun settles & the crane flies

Sometimes I watch the men soldiering home
       like they've been to a wedding they've never had

       trailing ribbons of paper from the burn of the machine
& on the women from workshop number nine

plastic confetti sprinkled in their hair
       like tiny little confessions floating behind

       One of our small perks is the after-shift dinners
boiled rice, & bok choy & dry fish heads

which my HR lady tells me is far better
       than what they normally get

       but little am I to know, I'm merely transposed:
a colon sent from the board to point the way ahead

In nine solid months and forty-five thousand fish heads
       we've reached all targets; we've out performed

    Kim Yung Boiled Meat Sticks
    Emperor Wu's Golden Fish Cakes

        Yes, indeed it's a miracle. The trick, of course
is in the distribution & getting them to appreciate

that only milk from free-range Western cows
        could settle the stomach of the Chinese working man

        could enrich the Ch'i so early in the morning
could steady the hands on the lathe

&, above all, making it available on bicycle carts
        outside every single factory in every single province

        Cream of Feng Shui
        Awaken the Tiger Within

        A yoghurt for the enlightened
        Free Range, healthy and keeps you slim

        & I wonder, as my term comes to an end, as I sit here
listening to each section manager praising my achievements

& the flowers & the toasts at the banquet table
        what they will think of the next face

        whether they will see him
as a traffic light or a conveyor belt

or a chair
        or even a cart

THICK END OF A CAMEL'S TAIL

Gobi creeps into big cities
flecks under human nails

she has her way of smoothing things
down to the nature of themselves
her hard glass grain like blood hungry mosquitoes

purple-haired housewives
in Saturday-starched window-shopping dresses

fit for an all night & day *Ganbei* wedding in fifteen pearl embroidered
wedding gowns
& a dowry fit for a chairman

but when they finally stumble home
barefoot in the pitch

giggling like foxes
heels swinging
ribbons of cigarette smoke float
like ghostly Christian halos

& when the Bactrian camel snorts for summer
Mr. Hua is still bicycling after all these years

he chews my tender lamb skewers
milk-fed on the Tarim basin
(where Beijing's tested atom bombs)

he loves to hear himself humming revolutionary songs
above the wallop & squeal of Benz & Beemer

diesel gives his shashlik just the right Atheist bite

he's pedalling to the Executive Council
behind banners & slogans & waves
to Ayi Lui with the peonies & roses & apple blossoms

as the lamb unfolds on his pointed tongue
he wipes his crystal-sewn eyes

& he stumbles into his conference hall
where he who knows who wags for whom

BLACK SKIES

The sun bottoms out
and they rise again,

air-tumbling whorls,
screaming four-letter words.

When our backs are turned
they go straight for the warm blood,

dying their beaks
in our carbon dioxide,

clicking their beaks
like mad scissors.

Joseph says their magic is in the feathers,
he calls them quills that ink the skies.

I say, strange they bleed cold.
But, Ah—respite,

he with the bow and arrow,
he with the eyes

in the back of his head,
he with the illusion of time.

MANCHURIAN FOG

Beijing December.
Clouds like steel wool,
buildings buffeted all along the Dong Wen Men,
ravaged traffic and smokestack-snowflakes
swirl like the aftermath of a nuclear storm;
all this before lunch, all this before the fog.
The world is almost visible,
living shadows dulled by frosted glass.
But here in your garden, the bamboo creaks,
and the cars become the breath of the city,
soft and harmless, like rain upon the tiles.

The noodles you serve are hot and sharp and
taste of your distant mountain homeland,
of the pine trees and the coarse flour
in your mother's kitchen
of the wood from her chopping board.

You suck your noodles like a great heron
his worms, splattering sauce
over your new pink blouse, and when you smile,
your teeth have turned blood red.

And now the world disappears again,

and your eyes dark as burned charcoal
and you throb like an incinerator in my head.

BARBERS

In 1915 I carted
combs, scissors, razors, clippers,
ear-cleaners & Brilliantine in slippers.
In Autumn, this same alley
was littered with hair
& leaves & chicken bone.

We barbers had a monopoly
on the head business
in the good old days.

If you weren't sporting
a Manchu Queue
we'd report you,
& off with your offending head.

Now barber shops line
alleys from Harbin to Shentou,
& red & white candy poles
make you dizzy;
& to truck drivers, salesmen,
sailors, chancellors
on the fly
country girls offer quick head
with one hand on a tube
of Johnson's baby oil.

But enough chit-chat.
Let me finish my chicken soup.

ADVANCED TREE PLANTING

Comrade Fa says:

Grassroots
democratic politics
is like water:

You have to channel it
to stop the flooding:

The people have to know
they're getting something

for all their back-breaking work.

SEEPAGE

& when you Piotr stared at me unflinching point blank
offered me a malt whiskey with or without a splash
your wife puckering new lips on champagne

said it's all leeching under the foundations
can't let the shareholders know or the factory would close
I just smiled back & cheered our good health—

The world was big & cancer was everywhere
in the meat, in the bread, the sky, the unflinching earth
only in Iceland will the volcanoes get you

& then there was factory kingpin Ying
with the blue phone glued to his ear—
he who rose from the communist earth

through the state-owned fields of wild flowers
past the guards of imperialism
into the bright future of capitalism

He who bought a house for his father
then down the line all the way to his second
no, third, cousin, uncle to his sister's second half-brother

    No one outdoes the law
    No one fulfils all moral obligations
    What the hell do we have lawyers for?

To find a way in without arousing suspicion
Along the way, be a dog if you need to wag
Be a whore if you need to get fucked

Above all, let nothing get in the way of your own hands of progress
One day sooner or later you'll need your own whore
It helps to break the monotony

& thus it was, came to be
that effluents surpassed basic constituents to life
Jupiter coming out of the other end of the tap

leaking like an old man's dribble
in his dirty underpants
& you both said

by the time anyone noticed you'd be retired
enjoying life, a garden of herbs & flowers
good food somewhere on a Pacific island

with parrots & deep sea swordfish &
clear blue cloudless skies
until the final day of passing

That night I was all fuzzy on vodka
as a girl with watermelon breasts
almost screwed me half to death

KEY

I might have been a radio, once—
collector or broadcaster
of selective sounds and tones,
I was a rambler of definitive points.

Some listened, most didn't.
Except in the car
where you couldn't turn me off.

Even in the parking garage
with the key jangling in your palm,
the chain twirling a disco ball.

It was then you said:
Don't you think we've had enough?
And you were right, of course.
There are only so many things you can say.

Sometimes you'd purse your lips,
clasping your purse like a wall, asking:
Do you want to tell the whole world?

Which was rhetorical.
These were the only sounds
that moved me to bee-static,

a slow whir that rang in my ears,
these, and that look in your eye
which was enough to put an end to most things.
But that was so long ago, before we went public.

It is worthy of remark that a belief constantly inculcated during the early years of life, whilst the brain is impressible, appears to acquire almost the nature of an instinct; and the very essence of an instinct is that it is followed independently of reason.

—Charles Darwin

WALL

This is the wall that contains history, he says,
kicking the brick with his boot.

Without her we would have become
a kingdom of small-thinking.

She has made us, contained us, distilled us
into a hard liquid, the protectors of seas and rivers;

has given us our edge over the encroaching barbarians
who incessantly beat at the gate.

This is the wall that holds in innocence, he says,
the purest nature of ourselves.

She is the only man-made structure
you can see from the moon.

Isn't she a wonder?

No Birds

~

The need for illusion is deep.

—Saul Bellow

No Birds

Early Shanghai mornings, window unzipped,
Hard tinny noises titter & trill & honk,
Shatter & ripple, yet, nowhere do sea birds skim:

No trash-pan kittiwakes, no lonesome terns fading
In mussel-caught pinpricks of sky dust,
Not a single sandpiper clowning carnival eights.

The wind smells burnt, sulphur-singed hot,
Charcoaled, as if he has been lying about everything,
Entirely unattended on the smoke-oil steel of wok.

Some Tarzan cleans the dizzy horizon with dirty rags,
Arcs pendulous on a single thread of corded hope.
Minutes later, memory wiped, window squeezed tight.

Inside, pigeons squirt bombs from the ceiling,
Grebes nest in my hair, a peacock struts the kitchen pecking crumbs
& the fattest phoenix of them all sits right here in the bath,

Preening, plashing away all that murky ash and dust.

Hear it? She's singing, as if in heaven.

TAISHAN MOUNTAIN

On Taishan Mountain behind the fog
we wait for first glimpses of dawn.

It's here, hovering on China's precipice,
the Chairman proclaims the East is Red,

deems himself ruler of all he beholds.
I'm standing right beside him.

We've just fought a war, he's so thin,
and he has this steely glint

as if he's stumbled across some great illumination.
It's a moment of connection with the universe,

a revelation beyond normal human comprehension,
something to make history, like Einstein

unravelling the universal laws
of energy and mass and motion.

In this moment I know nothing will ever be the same again.
I know he has to tear the world apart at the seams,

fold it back upon itself to find his true place in it.
Everything for love, he says.

He breathes in, as if trying to capture the last
essence of olden sky, and as often, he considers

one of his heroes, Karl Marx, and what that bearded
wonder might have said on a day such as this,

in a definitive moment such as this.
And you won't believe it,

but he turns from the spectacle
of nature illuminating before us,

the hills, the valley, the forest below and faces me full-on,
grabs my head in his smoky hands and plants a huge, wet kiss on my lips,

then says: We've all got to move on. You know, Richard,
you've got to get rid of that damn moustache.

Xiao Hong's Great Leap Forward

Tradition says: Women are grass.
Tradition says: Women are born to be stepped on.

We burn our schools and books to the ground.
Teacher Liu looks like a stork in a dunce hat.
Red Guard Pang beats him silly with bamboo.

Chairman says: Brothers and sisters are equal.
Chairman says: Women uphold half the sky.

Hot fire is red, blood is red.
We don't need entertainment.
Our theatre is played out on the streets.

Chairman says: Without destruction no construction.
Chairman says: Be red. Don't be an expert.

When I'm twenty-one I dance chest-to-chest
with Chairman in the park.
My heart leaps for joy, I nearly faint.

Chairman says: Melt hot steel in your back garden
Chairman says: Stoke a furnace beneath your apple tree.

And we become scarecrows, we kill
the sparrows for our Great Helmsmen,
for they are the scourge of the fields.

Chairman says: Revolution is not a dinner party.
Chairman says: Make the future new!

Comrade Pang lights Chairman's Panda cigarette.
Up close he smells of lotus flowers.
I wish I could kiss him on the mouth.

Chairman says: He is the sun that never sets.
Chairman says: These are the best years of our lives.

And my heart grows
redder and redder and redder.

RANGOON

for John Adolphus Pope

City at the end of strife
far from the cry of borstal whippersnappers.

I do remember the milky tea
& the triangular cucumber sandwiches.

Mother calls her ladies
an outpost of the foreign legion

& pours with abandon
as if this may be her last cup yet.

She offers slices of homemade fruitcake
& waves away the flies.

Father sells opium to appease her majesty, Queen Victoria
and please poor Chinese fishermen.

Sarah and I play croquet on the lawn.
(She always wins.)

A hundred years from now a junta will oppose
everything we've made from scratch.

I say Praise the Industrial Revolution
but observe the gaping hole in our constitution.

Monkeys can scream all they want at the pagoda
burning on the hill, but the moon is still gone.

What an embarrassment.
You know, you can never please the natives.

BASE PAIRS

old Shanghai drags her feet
from screw top jars
so she can avoid the bite
just to have a pee
comes in slow spurts
when taxis brim
with umbrellas
but buildings still rise
the elevator
never smiles
& your tealeaves
the seventeenth floor
to cook a steamed fish!
for the pan to heat
the gas is always grumbling
of the hammer drill in apartment 1804
of Tibetan Yaks up there
with their green and white bricks
they jostle & prod & poke
my, my you're fatter than ever, or
is your granddaughter still not married?
you're about to win again

sips hot tea
holds herself for hours
of the heartless bathroom
which anyway
on rainy days
men beat each other
senseless
& the woman who mans
with a flick of the switch
except when your grocery bags burst
spill all over
oh the trouble
the time it takes to wait
the water to bubble
& the thump and grind
sounds like a herd
at sunset Auntie and Uncle arrive
of Mahjiang
saying things like:
that's not your real hair colour, is it? or
but you rub your hands together
& soon there will be all this

SUZIE LAM SCORNS THE HAPPY MARRIAGE DATING AGENCY

Toes

Twenty-something Suzie Lam, my dirty-weekend fling, tells me identity is a fickle thing, says everyone grows up wanting to be a cowboy or an astronaut, when all we really need is to cross a river without getting wet. Suzie wiggles her black-nail-polish toes and spoons herself Häagen-Dazs straight from the tub.

For some reason she likes to eat in bed.

Husbands

If you don't know who you are how can you go find a husband who can walk straight on two feet? When you want to grow up, you've got to shed your skin. Yes, I've become quite a snake she says, and hisses. In my case it was a shabby straw hat, parents who couldn't write or read and a cat named Ding Dong who was afraid of mice. In Szechuan everything trembles beneath your feet so there's nothing really to stand on. Hong Kong, on the other hand, is built on promises.

There's a dribble of ice cream on her chin and I'd love to lick it right off, only I know she wouldn't go for that.

Words

I used to keep a diary, all my history narrowed down to a thin disguise.
Now only what's still to come serves a purpose. At the dating agency
there's no such thing as a happy marriage. Normally the men arrive in a
taxi, sometimes with a bunch of peonies, hair greased back into a quip.
They know if I'm not interested, I just tell them let's just be friends then.
I've never finished a single date.

She licks her fingers, fluffs her pillow and stares at the fan on the ceiling.

Chatting

The QQ Chat Service is an excellent thing, the internet draws a higher
class of men. Most Chinese marriages are not built on love, you know, but
I'm not willing to compromise, not just yet.

Besides, I know you'd never leave your wife.

THE RIVER, ONCE

once she went to quench
then she went to scrub

now she collects dead toads
grinds them with cornmeal to feed her sows

once she ploughed the land
toiled with her face deep in dark soil

her back burning in hot sun
now she works in the paper mill

making laminated labels for the city
sundays she takes a out boat

not to take in the view or dream
but to gather plastic bags

now she drinks from water bottles
carted here all the way from the city

label reads: pure filtered glacier water
and says it's drawn from a mountain

it reminds her of a spring
at the foot of a sleeping dragon

SEAFILL

Remember the birds
for their seasons

ecumenical spires, nails
hanging on country dales

clanging of Sunday sermons
falling asleep at the pyre, burning

the waste of reason wilted down
to the disfigured deposit

of carton, plastics & rind. Sea's bride
a floating PET as an island.

Last haven of migrations, soiled
footprint embossed eternal

in a billion bottle caps:
three in the landfill

two in the hand
one on the glorious ocean.

[*   *   *]

The world is watercolour blue.

We tack up the coast
in our chrome-polished eighteen wheeler, she and I

and our millions of lives encased in slatted hives,
layers of egg and worm and honeycomb.

She's white-washed white almost ceramic,
laid-out-for-dinner in that dandelion dress.

I'm greased back in hand-me-down dungarees,
beguiled by her whiteness and hungry for sunlight.

We're both growing electric from the inside.
At Las Almendras the full-fruited almond trees whisper

and our bees are listening, dancing dutifully,
filling in the blanks with sucrose.

Three miles downwind she and I breathe sea
barefoot among the dunes.

She wonders if the missing nut-brown tourists
are across the other side of the world

and if a song or a word
has carried them elsewhere.

This is the first time I understand that our bees are mindless slaves
toiling for the world's sweetness,

but these afternoons in a beach house we paramour on chardonnay
reclining, salt-soaked and shimmering in sand crystals like diamonds.

On the fourth, before turning back into the panhandle highway,
we find our hives abandoned, beeless.

There is not a yellow soul in the trees, in the flesh of the skies
or scattered on the earth's surface.

She says now they're free and palms the last queen,
pops its head like a ripe berry on a twig

hums a midday song of remembrance and loss
and I curse the scientists for what they have done to the trees.

The world is watercolour blue.

ACKNOWLEDGEMENTS

The Propaganda Factory, or Speaking of Trees was originally published in 2011 as an Argotist E-book. I am grateful to Jeffrey Side for his faith in the work, and for allowing this new edition to be published.

Many thanks to the following publications:

Poets and Artists, MiPOradio, nth position, Stirring, Pirene's Fountain, Rumble, Ducts Journal, Lantern Review, Poets' Corner, October Babies, Mobius: The Journal of Social Change

"Thick End of a Camel's Tail," "Seepage," "No Birds," and "The River, Once," were previously published in *Upholding Half the Sky* (GOSS 183: Casa Menedez, 2010)

S P U Y T E N   D U Y V I L
Meeting Eyes Bindery
Triton
Lithic Scatter

Made in the USA
Monee, IL
07 July 2026

56551557R00037